Taste of Home's
Favorite Brand Name Recipes
2007

Taste of Home Books

Enjoy over 350 Recipes from the Brand Names You Trust the Most!

"COMFORTING" is just one word that describes the mouthwatering recipes found in this edition of *Taste of Home's Favorite Brand Name Recipes.* Whether you're looking for a bubbling casserole, aromatic bread or steaming soup, this heartwarming collection is sure to help you create family-pleasing meals throughout the year.

Taste of Home, America's No. 1 cooking magazine, is known for sharing satisfying recipes that are ideal for home cooks. Not only do those dishes come together easily, but they're guaranteed to turn out right every time…and the items in this book are no exception! That's because each dish was handpicked by a home economist from the *Taste of Home* Test Kitchen.

Best of all, you won't waste time or money looking for hard-to-find ingredients or purchasing unique items you'll use only occasionally. The lip-smacking recipes found here call for kitchen staples you likely have on hand.

Tortellini Carbonara

Cream of the Crop

You can feel confident when preparing these dishes because they feature the name-brand foods you trust the most. In fact, many of the recipes actually came from the brands you've welcomed into your home for years.

For instance, when we wanted to publish a creamy seafood party-starter, we selected Hot Artichoke and Tuna Spread from StarKist®…the folks who know tuna best (see page 20 in the Appetizers & Snacks chapter).

When we wanted to spice things up with Italian flair, we chose Contadina's® zesty Eggplant Parmesan (as seen on page 46 in the Side Dishes chapter). We also selected Greek Island Shrimp Pita Pockets from the talented cooks at French's® for some great Mediterranean flavors (the details are in the Sandwiches chapter on page 90).

When it came to main courses, the Jennie-O Turkey Store® was a great source for items such as Turkey

Pot Pie (check out page 148) and Turkey with Herb Dumplings (found on page 160). See the poultry main dishes as well as beefy entrées and pork favorites starting on page 127.

More to Chew On

In addition to unbeatable appetizers, sensational side dishes and savory main courses, you'll find plenty of sweet treats from Nestle® Toll House®, Duncan Hines® and others. There are also dozens of refreshing salads, unbeatable biscuits and old-fashioned coffee cakes … all sure to be winners in your home.

This edition of *Taste of Home's Favorite Brand Name Recipes* will take you from the start of a family meal to the finish. You won't believe how easy it is to create crowd-pleasing menus that keep your gang racing to the supper table night after night.

Not only will this book's enormous selection of recipes and the 100-plus photographs help you solve your dinnertime dilemmas, but specific chapters and two indexes make it easy to find the perfect recipe at a moment's notice.

Buffalo Chicken Salad Italiano

Tropical Sunshine Cake

Finding a Recipe

See page 213 for a general index that lists every recipe by food category, major ingredient and/or cooking method. It's a great tool to help you decide what to prepare for dinner.

For instance, if you have some beef in the refrigerator that you'd like to serve tonight, turn to "beef" in the general index. You'll find several delicious options to chose from.

The alphabetical index is another useful reference. Starting on page 221, it helps you quickly locate your family's favorite recipes by name.

We hope the 2007 edition of *Taste of Home's Favorite Brand Name Recipes* becomes your most valuable kitchen helper. It was a pleasure bringing it to you. Enjoy!

Appetizers & Snacks

Texas-Style Stuffed Pizza Bread

(pictured at left)

> 1 package (13.8 ounces) refrigerated pizza crust
> 1/3 cup *French's® Gourmayo™* Smoked Chipotle Light Mayonnaise
> 1/2 pound sliced deli roast beef
> 1/4 pound sliced mozzarella or Jack cheese
> 1 jar (7-1/2 ounces) roasted red peppers, drained and sliced
> 1 cup sautéed onions*
> 1 teaspoon olive oil
> 1 teaspoon dried oregano leaves
> 1 teaspoon minced garlic

*To sauté onions, cook 1-1/2 cups sliced onions in 1 tablespoon oil for 5 minutes or until tender.

1. Heat oven to 425°F. Roll pizza dough into 13×10-inch rectangle on floured work surface. Spread mayonnaise evenly on dough. Layer roast beef and cheese on dough, overlapping slices, leaving a 1-inch border around edges. Top with peppers and onion.

2. Fold one-third of dough toward center from long edge of rectangle. Fold second side toward center enclosing filling. Tightly pinch long edge and ends to seal. Place seam-side down on greased baking sheet.

3. Brush with oil; sprinkle with oregano and garlic. Cut shallow slits crosswise along top of dough, spacing 3 inches apart. Bake 18 to 20 minutes or until deep golden brown. Remove to rack; cool slightly. Serve warm.   *Makes 12 servings*

Clockwise from top left: *Beef and Veggie Flatbread (p. 14), Spanish Omelet (p. 12), Texas-Style Stuffed Pizza Bread and Bacon-Wrapped BBQ Chicken (p. 16)*

Frittata Stuffed Mushrooms

(pictured at right)

> 30 (2- to 2-1/2-inch) button or cremini mushrooms, stems removed and caps wiped clean
> 2 tablespoons olive oil, divided
> 1 teaspoon salt
> 1/2 teaspoon pepper, divided
> 1/2 cup chopped onion
> 1 teaspoon minced garlic
> 1/2 package (10 ounces) frozen chopped spinach, thawed and squeezed dry
> 3/4 teaspoon dried oregano
> 1/2 cup plus 2 tablespoons shredded Parmesan cheese, divided
> 1 tablespoon dried breadcrumbs
> 2 eggs, beaten
> 1/3 cup half-and-half cream

1. Preheat oven to 400°F. Lightly grease 2 large baking pans. Combine 1 tablespoon oil, salt and 1/4 teaspoon pepper in medium bowl; mix well. Add mushroom caps; toss to coat. Arrange mushrooms, rounded side down, on baking sheets; set aside.

2. Heat remaining 1 tablespoon oil in large skillet over medium heat. Add onion, garlic and remaining 1/4 teaspoon pepper. Cook 5 minutes. Add spinach and oregano; cook 2 to 3 minutes. Remove from heat; stir in 1/2 cup cheese and bread crumbs. Cool 15 minutes.

3. Combine eggs and half-and-half cream in medium bowl; mix well. Stir in spinach mixture. Spoon filling into mushroom cavities. Sprinkle with remaining 2 tablespoons cheese. Bake 10 to 15 minutes or until mushrooms are tender. Serve warm or at room temperature.   *Makes 30 mushrooms*

Onion Swiss Cheese Bites

> 2 cups *French's®* French Fried Onions
> 6 (1/2-inch-thick) slices firm white bread
> 1/3 cup shredded Swiss cheese
> 1 package (3 ounces) cream cheese
> 2 tablespoons butter
> 1 tablespoon *French's®* Spicy Brown Mustard
> 2 egg whites

1. Preheat oven to 350°F. Place French Fried Onions in plastic bag; crush with rolling pin. Transfer to sheet of waxed paper. Trim crusts from bread. Cut each slice diagonally into 4 triangles; set aside.

2. Combine cheeses, butter and mustard in microwave-safe bowl. Heat on HIGH 1 minute; stir. Heat on HIGH 30 seconds longer or until cheese melts, stirring until smooth.

3. Beat egg whites in medium bowl until stiff. Fold 1/4 of beaten egg whites into cheese mixture to lighten. Fold in remaining egg whites. Dip each bread triangle into cheese mixture, then into crushed onions to coat evenly. Place triangles on foil-lined baking sheet. Bake 10 minutes or until golden.   *Makes 24 triangles*

Veg•All® Party Dip

> 2 cans (15 ounces each) VEG•ALL® Original Mixed Vegetables, drained
> 1-1/2 cups sour cream
> 1 package (10 ounces) frozen chopped spinach, cooked according to package directions and drained
> 1/2 cup mayonnaise
> 1/4 cup chopped green onions
> 1 envelope (1 ounce) dried onion soup mix

In large mixing bowl, combine all ingredients, mixing well. Cover; refrigerate for 4 hours. Transfer to serving bowl. Serve with chips or crackers.   *Makes 4 cups*

BelGioioso® Fontina Melt

> 1 loaf Italian or French bread
> 2 fresh tomatoes, cubed
> Basil leaves, julienned
> BELGIOIOSO® Fontina Cheese, sliced

Cut bread lengthwise into halves. Top each half with tomatoes and sprinkle with basil. Top with BelGioioso Fontina Cheese. Place in oven at 350°F for 10 to 12 minutes or until cheese is golden brown.   *Makes 6 to 8 servings*

Frittata Stuffed Mushrooms

Spicy Cheddar Stuffed Tomatoes

Spicy Cheddar Stuffed Tomatoes

(pictured above)

    6 medium tomatoes
    2 cups (8 ounces) Sargento® Fancy Sharp
        Cheddar Shredded Cheese, divided
    1 can (4 ounces) diced green chilies, well
        drained
  1/4 teaspoon dried oregano leaves, crushed
  1/4 teaspoon minced garlic
    6 tablespoons sour cream
    3 green onions, sliced
        Breadsticks for serving

1. Preheat oven to 325°F. Grease 11×7-inch baking dish. Cut 1/2-inch slice from top of each tomato; scoop out pulp and seeds, leaving 1/4-inch shell (save pulp for another use such as salads or sauces).

2. Invert tomatoes on paper towel-lined plate; let drain 20 minutes.

3. Combine 1-1/2 cups cheese, chilies, oregano and garlic in medium bowl.

4. Using large spoon, stuff tomato shells with cheese mixture.

5. Arrange tomato shells in prepared dish. Bake 20 minutes. Top with sour cream, remaining 1/2 cup cheese and green onions. Serve with breadsticks.

Makes 6 first-course servings

Artichokes with Dijon Mayonnaise

    2 DOLE® Fresh Artichokes
        Lemon juice
  2/3 cup fat-free or reduced-fat mayonnaise
    2 tablespoons finely chopped DOLE® Green
        Onions
    1 tablespoon lemon juice
    1 tablespoon Dijon-style mustard
  1/4 teaspoon prepared horseradish

• Wash artichokes; trim stems. Cut off 1 inch from tops of artichokes; cut off sharp leaf tips. Brush cut edges with lemon juice to prevent browning.

• Place artichokes in large pot of boiling water (artichokes should be completely covered with water).

• Cook, covered, 25 to 35 minutes or until leaf pulls off easily from artichoke. Drain artichokes upside down 10 to 15 minutes.

• Stir together mayonnaise, green onions, 1 tablespoon lemon juice, mustard and horseradish in small bowl.

• Spoon dip into serving bowl; serve with artichokes. *Makes 6 servings*

Curry Mayonnaise: Omit mustard; stir in 2 teaspoons curry powder and 1 teaspoon chutney.

Garlic Mayonnaise: Omit mustard; stir in 2 garlic cloves, minced, and 2 tablespoons fresh minced parsley.

Herb Mayonnaise: Omit mustard; stir in 2 tablespoons nonfat milk and 1/2 teaspoon each: dill weed, dried basil leaves, crushed and dried rosemary, crushed.

Tex-Mex Potato Skins

(pictured below)

3 hot baked potatoes, split lengthwise
3/4 cup (3 ounces) shredded Cheddar or pepper
   Jack cheese
1-1/3 cups *French's*® French Fried Onions, divided
1/4 cup chopped green chilies
1/4 cup crumbled cooked bacon
   Salsa and sour cream

1. Preheat oven to 350°F. Scoop out inside of potatoes, leaving 1/4-inch shells. Reserve inside of potatoes for another use.

2. Arrange potato halves on baking sheet. Top with cheese, *2/3 cup* French Fried Onions, chilies and bacon.

3. Bake 15 minutes or until heated through and cheese is melted. Cut each potato half crosswise into thirds. Serve topped with salsa, sour cream and remaining onions.   *Makes 18 appetizer servings*

Tip: To bake potatoes quickly, microwave at HIGH 10 to 12 minutes or until tender.

Variation: For added Cheddar flavor, substitute *French's*® **Cheddar French Fried Onions** for the original flavor.

Fresh Garden Dip

1-1/2 cups fat-free or reduced-fat mayonnaise
1-1/2 cups shredded DOLE® Carrots
   1 cup finely chopped DOLE® Broccoli
1/3 cup finely chopped DOLE® Green Onions
   2 teaspoons dill weed
1/4 teaspoon garlic powder
   DOLE® Broccoli or Cauliflower, cut into
      florets, DOLE® Carrots or Celery, sliced

• Stir together mayonnaise, carrots, broccoli, green onions, dill and garlic powder in medium bowl.

• Spoon into serving bowl. Cover; chill 1 hour or overnight. Serve with assorted fresh vegetables. Refrigerate any leftovers in airtight container.
     Makes 14 servings

Tex-Mex Potato Skins

Indian-Spiced Walnuts (p. 18) and Southwest-Spiced Walnuts

Southwest-Spiced Walnuts

(pictured above)

2 cups California walnuts
1 tablespoon sugar
1 teaspoon sea salt
1/2 teaspoon garlic powder
1/2 teaspoon ground cumin
1/4 teaspoon cayenne pepper
1 tablespoon walnut oil

Preheat oven to 375°F. Plunge walnuts into a pot of boiling water, turn off heat and let stand 2 minutes; drain. Spread walnuts on baking sheet and roast 10 minutes. Measure seasonings in a small bowl and stir to combine. Heat oil in a skillet. Add walnuts and toss 1 minute. Add seasoning mixture and toss until walnuts are well coated. Cool on a paper towel.

Makes 2 cups

Favorite recipe from **Walnut Marketing Board**

Bacon-Wrapped BBQ Chicken

(pictured on page 6)

8 chicken tender strips, patted dry (about 1 pound)
1/2 teaspoon paprika or cumin (optional)
8 slices bacon
1/2 cup barbecue sauce

1. Preheat broiler. Line broiler pan with foil and set aside.

2. Sprinkle chicken strips with seasoning, if desired. Wrap each chicken strip with one slice of bacon in spiral; place on broiler pan.

3. Broil chicken 4 minutes; turn and broil 2 minutes. Remove from oven and brush with 1/4 cup barbecue sauce. Broil 2 minutes. Remove from oven, turn over chicken strips and baste with remaining barbecue sauce. Broil 2 minutes. Serve warm.

Makes 4 servings

Mini Italian Meatballs

1 pound lean ground beef
1/4 cup finely diced onion
3 teaspoons HERB-OX® beef flavored bouillon
1/2 cup Italian-style seasoned bread crumbs
1 egg, slightly beaten
1/4 cup pizza sauce
1 (10-3/4-ounce) can Italian Herb tomato soup, undiluted
1 cup shredded mozzarella cheese
Vegetable oil, for frying

In bowl, combine ground beef, onion, bouillon, bread crumbs, egg and pizza sauce. Shape meat mixture into 48 (1/2-inch) meatballs. In large skillet, in a small amount of oil, brown meatballs until lightly browned on all sides. Place meatballs in a single layer in a 13×9-inch baking dish. Spoon soup over meatballs and sprinkle with cheese. Cover and bake at 350°F for 20 to 30 minutes or until meat is cooked through. *Makes 48 servings*

Meatball Making: For 48 meatballs of equal size, shape meat mixture into an 8×6-inch rectangle on waxed paper. Cut into 1-inch squares; roll each square into a ball.

Zesty Pesto Cheese Spread and Dip

(pictured below)

2 packages (8 ounces each) cream cheese, softened
1 cup shredded mozzarella cheese
1 cup chopped fresh basil or parsley
1/2 cup grated Parmesan cheese
1/2 cup pine nuts, toasted
1/3 cup *French's® Gourmayo™* Caesar Ranch Mayonnaise
1 teaspoon minced garlic

1. Combine all ingredients in food processor. Cover and process until smooth and well blended.

2. Spoon pesto spread into serving bowl or crock. Spread on crackers or serve with vegetable crudités.   *Makes 12 (1/4-cup) servings*

Tip: To toast pine nuts, place nuts on baking sheet. Bake at 350°F for 8 to 10 minutes or until lightly golden or microwave on HIGH (100%) 1 minute.

Double Cheese Crab Dip

1 cup PACE® Picante Sauce or Chunky Salsa
1 teaspoon chili powder
1 package (8 ounces) cream cheese, softened
1 can (8 ounces) refrigerated pasteurized crabmeat
1 cup shredded Cheddar cheese (4 ounces)
1/4 cup sliced pitted ripe olives
Pita bread, cut into wedges, tortilla chips or assorted cut-up fresh vegetables

1. Mix picante sauce and chili powder. Spread cream cheese in 9-inch pie plate. Top with picante sauce mixture, crabmeat, Cheddar cheese, olives and additional picante sauce.

2. Bake at 350°F. for 15 minutes or until hot. Serve with pita, chips or vegetables for dipping.
Makes about 3 cups

Time-Saving Tip: To soften cream cheese, remove from wrapper. On microwave-safe plate, microwave on HIGH 15 seconds.

Zesty Pesto Cheese Spread and Dip

Peppery Brie en Croûte

(pictured at right)

2 (4-ounce) packages crescent roll dough
1 (8-ounce) wheel Brie cheese
2 tablespoons TABASCO® brand Green Pepper
    Sauce
1 egg, beaten
    Crackers

Preheat oven to 375°F. Work crescent roll dough into thin circle large enough to completely wrap cheese. Place cheese in center of dough circle. Prick top of cheese several times with fork. Slowly pour 1 tablespoon TABASCO® Green Pepper Sauce over top of cheese. Let stand briefly for sauce to sink in.

Add remaining 1 tablespoon TABASCO® Green Pepper Sauce, pricking cheese several more times with fork. (Some sauce will run over side of cheese.) Bring edges of dough over top of cheese, working it together to completely cover cheese. Brush edges with beaten egg and seal. Bake about 10 minutes, following directions on crescent roll package. ·(Do not overbake, as cheese will run.) Serve immediately with crackers.

Makes 8 to 10 servings

Pastry Puffs with Goat Cheese and Spinach

1 (12-ounce) package BOB EVANS® Original
    Links
30 to 40 leaves fresh spinach
1 (17-3/4-ounce) package frozen puff pastry
    sheets, thawed according to package
    directions
1/3 cup goat cheese*
3 tablespoons Dijon mustard

For a milder flavor, substitute plain or herb cream cheese for goat cheese.

Cook sausage in large skillet until browned. Drain on paper towels; let cool. Steam spinach; let cool. Preheat oven to 375°F. Cut 1 pastry sheet evenly into 9 squares. Cut 5 additional squares from second sheet (remaining pastry may be refrozen for future use). Stretch or roll squares slightly to form rectangles. Line each rectangle with 2 or 3 spinach leaves, leaving 1/4 inch on 1 short end to seal edges. Spread about 1 teaspoon goat cheese over spinach; spread 1/2 teaspoon mustard over goat cheese.

Arrange sausage across short end and roll up pastry and filling, pressing to seal edges. Place on *ungreased* baking sheet, seam sides down. Bake 14 to 16 minutes or until golden. Cut each puff into halves or thirds. Refrigerate leftovers.

Makes 28 to 42 appetizers

Note: Pastry puffs may be made ahead and refrigerated overnight or frozen up to 1 month. Reheat in oven when ready to serve.

Hot Artichoke and Tuna Spread

1 (3-ounce) STARKIST Flavor Fresh Pouch® Tuna
    (Albacore)
1 jar (12 ounces) marinated artichoke hearts,
    drained
1 cup shredded mozzarella cheese
1/2 cup grated Parmesan cheese
1/4 cup chopped canned green chilies
1 to 2 cloves garlic
2 to 3 tablespoons mayonnaise
1 tablespoon minced green onion
    Hot pepper sauce to taste
    French bread or assorted crackers

In food processor bowl with metal blade, place all ingredients except bread. Process until well blended but not puréed. Transfer mixture to ovenproof serving dish. Bake, uncovered, in 350°F oven about 30 minutes or until mixture is golden. Serve hot with French bread. *Makes 12 servings*

Note: This mixture may be baked in small hollowed bread shell. Wrap in foil; bake as above. Open top of foil last 5 minutes of baking.

Helpful Hint

When preparing appetizers to eat before a meal choose one to two selections to serve, allowing three to four servings per person.

Peppery Brie en Croûte

Fruited Lamb Salad

(pictured at right)

   3 cups cooked American lamb, cubed or cut into slices
   3 cups cooked brown and wild rice, chilled
1-1/2 cups sliced strawberries
1-1/2 cups orange slices, cubed
  3/4 cup green grapes
  1/2 cup sliced bananas
  1/4 cup walnuts
   2 tablespoons honey
   2 tablespoons lemon juice
   1 tablespoon orange juice
  12 large Romaine lettuce leaves

Combine lamb, rice, fruit and nuts in large bowl. Combine honey, lemon juice and orange juice in small bowl; toss with lamb mixture. Refrigerate. Serve on lettuce leaves.   *Makes 12 servings*

Favorite recipe from **American Lamb Council**

Tomato & Mozzarella Salad with Sun-Dried Tomato Dressing

DRESSING
1/3 cup water
1/4 cup *French's®* Worcestershire Sauce
1/4 cup balsamic vinegar
1/4 cup sun-dried tomatoes packed in oil, drained
  2 tablespoons *French's®* Honey Dijon Mustard
  2 cloves garlic, minced
1/2 cup olive oil

SALAD
  6 cups washed and torn mixed salad greens
  2 large ripe tomatoes, sliced
  8 ounces fresh mozzarella cheese,* sliced
  1 bunch asparagus, trimmed and blanched**
  1 tablespoon minced fresh basil leaves

Look for fresh mozzarella in the deli section of your supermarket.

**To blanch asparagus, cook asparagus in boiling water 2 minutes. Drain and rinse with cold water.*

Place water, Worcestershire, vinegar, sun-dried tomatoes, mustard and garlic in blender or food processor. Cover and process until well blended. Gradually add oil in steady stream, processing until smooth. Set aside.

Place salad greens on large platter. Arrange tomatoes, cheese and asparagus on top. Sprinkle with basil. Serve with Dressing.
Makes 6 to 8 servings (about 1-1/2 cups dressing)

Chilled Steak and Mushroom Salad

  1 (12-ounce) boneless sirloin steak (2 inches thick)
  2 tablespoons MRS. DASH® STEAK GRILLING BLENDS™
1/2 pound mushrooms, sliced
1/2 cup sliced green onions
1/4 cup minced fresh parsley
  2 tablespoons olive oil
  1 tablespoon white wine vinegar
  2 teaspoons Dijon mustard
  1 teaspoon MRS. DASH® Lemon Pepper Seasoning Blend
  2 teaspoons fresh lemon juice
  1 teaspoon Worcestershire sauce
  1 cup sliced cherry tomatoes

Preheat broiler or grill to high heat.

Season both sides of steak with Mrs. Dash® Steak Grilling Blends™.

Cook steak to medium-rare, 4 to 5 minutes per side. Allow to cool slightly; refrigerate. After steak is chilled, slice into 1/4-inch-thick slices.

Combine mushrooms, green onions and parsley in large bowl.

Whisk together olive oil, vinegar, mustard, Mrs. Dash® Lemon Pepper Seasoning Blend, lemon juice and Worcestershire sauce.

Add steak to mushroom mixture and toss with dressing.

Garnish with cherry tomatoes. Serve cold with your favorite bread.   *Makes 4 servings*

Fruited Lamb Salad

Scalloped Apples & Onions

Scalloped Apples & Onions

(pictured above)

**1 medium onion, thinly sliced
4 tablespoons butter, melted, divided
5 red or green apples, cored and thinly sliced
8 ounces (1-1/2 cups) pasteurized process
     cheese, cut into small pieces, divided
2 cups** *French's®* **French Fried Onions, divided**

1. Preheat oven to 375°F. Sauté onion in 2 tablespoons butter in medium skillet over medium-high heat 3 minutes or until tender. Add apples and sauté 5 minutes or until apples are tender.

2. Stir 1 cup cheese, *1 cup* French Fried Onions and remaining melted butter into apple mixture. Transfer to greased 9-inch deep-dish pie plate.

3. Bake, uncovered, 20 minutes or until heated through. Top with remaining cheese and onions. Bake 5 minutes or until cheese is melted.
Makes 6 side-dish servings

Tip: To save time and cleanup, apple mixture may be baked in a heatproof skillet if desired. Wrap skillet handle in heavy-duty foil.

Variation: For added Cheddar flavor, substitute *French's®* *Cheddar French Fried Onions* for the original flavor.

Mushroom Ratatouille

**1 pound fresh white mushrooms
2 large onions (about 1 pound)
1 medium eggplant (1 pound)
2 medium zucchini (1 pound)
1 large sweet red bell pepper (about 8 ounces)
2 large ripe tomatoes (1 pound)
2 tablespoons olive oil
4 teaspoons finely chopped garlic
1 teaspoon Italian seasoning
3/4 teaspoon salt
1/2 teaspoon ground black pepper**

Cut mushrooms in thick slices; slice onions in wedges; cut eggplant, zucchini, red bell pepper and tomatoes in 1-inch cubes. In a large (12-inch) skillet (preferably nonstick), heat oil over medium heat. Add onions and garlic; cook and stir until lightly browned, about 4 minutes. Add mushrooms and eggplant; cook and stir until lightly browned, about 4 minutes. Add zucchini, bell pepper, tomatoes, Italian seasoning, salt and black pepper. Cover and cook, stirring occasionally, just until vegetables are tender, about 10 minutes. Serve in four grilled portabella caps on a bed of couscous, if desired.
Makes 6 to 8 servings (8 cups)

Favorite recipe from **Mushroom Council**

Bulgur with Onion

**1 tablespoon FILIPPO BERIO® Olive Oil
1 small onion, chopped
2-1/2 cups beef broth or chicken broth
6 ounces (about 1 cup) cracked bulgur wheat**

In large saucepan, heat olive oil over medium heat until hot. Add onion; cook and stir 3 to 5 minutes or until softened. Gradually add beef broth; bring to a boil. Stir in bulgur. Cover; reduce heat to low and simmer 25 minutes or until bulgur is tender and liquid is absorbed. *Makes 6 servings*

Savory Herb Roasted Potatoes

(pictured below)

2 pounds red potatoes, cut into wedges (about
     6 medium)
1-1/3 cups *French's®* Cheddar French Fried Onions or
     French's® French Fried Onions
1/4 cup parsley, minced
6 cloves garlic, halved
6 sprigs thyme or rosemary
2 tablespoons olive oil
1 teaspoon salt
1/4 teaspoon ground black pepper
2 ice cubes
1 large foil oven roasting bag

1. Toss all ingredients in large bowl. Open foil bag;
spoon potatoes into bag in an even layer. Seal bag
with tight double folds. Place bag on baking sheet.

2. Place bag on grill over medium-high heat. Cover
grill and cook 25 minutes until potatoes are tender,
turning bag over once.

3. Return bag to baking sheet and carefully cut top
of bag open. Sprinkle with additional French Fried
Onions if desired.   *Makes 4 to 6 servings*

Note: Too cold for outdoor grilling? Bake these
potatoes in a 450°F oven for 25 to 30 minutes.

Italian Green Bean Casserole

1 can (10-3/4 ounces) condensed cream of
     mushroom soup (low-fat or fat-free may be
     used)
1/2 cup milk
1-1/2 teaspoons soy sauce
     Black pepper to taste
2 cans (14.5 ounces each) or 1 can (28 ounces)
     ALLENS® Cut Italian Green Beans, drained
1-1/3 cups French-fried onions, divided

Preheat oven to 350°F. In a 1-1/2-quart casserole,
mix together soup, milk, soy sauce, pepper, Italian
green beans and 2/3 cup onions. Bake for
25 minutes, or until heated through; stir. Sprinkle
remaining onions on top. Bake 5 to 10 minutes, until
onions are golden.   *Makes 6 servings*

Savory Herb Roasted Potatoes

Scalloped Potatoes with Gorgonzola

(pictured at right)

1 (14-1/2-ounce) can chicken broth
1-1/2 cups whipping cream
4 teaspoons minced garlic
1-1/2 teaspoons dried sage leaves
1 cup BELGIOIOSO® Gorgonzola Cheese
2-1/4 pounds russet potatoes, peeled, halved and thinly sliced
Salt and pepper to taste

Preheat oven to 375°F. In medium heavy saucepan, simmer chicken broth, whipping cream, garlic and sage 5 minutes or until slightly thickened. Add BelGioioso® Gorgonzola Cheese and stir until melted. Remove from heat.

Place potatoes in large bowl and season with salt and pepper. Arrange half of potatoes in 13×9×2-inch glass baking dish. Pour half of cream mixture over top of potatoes. Repeat layers with remaining potatoes and cream mixture. Bake until potatoes are tender, about 1-1/4 hours. Let stand 15 minutes before serving. *Makes 8 servings*

Easy Summer Vegetable Medley

(pictured on page 44)

2 medium red or green bell peppers, cut into chunks
2 medium zucchini or summer squash, sliced lengthwise in half and then into thick slices
1 (12-ounce) box mushrooms, cleaned and cut into quarters
3 carrots, thinly sliced
1-1/3 cups *French's*® French Fried Onions or *French's*® Cheddar French Fried Onions
1/4 cup fresh basil, minced
2 tablespoons olive oil
Salt and pepper to taste
2 ice cubes
1 large foil oven roasting bag

1. Toss all ingredients in large bowl. Open foil bag; spoon mixture into bag in an even layer. Seal bag with tight double folds. Place bag on baking sheet.

2. Place bag on grill over medium-high heat. Cover grill and cook 15 minutes until vegetables are tender, turning bag over once.

. Return bag to baking sheet and carefully cut top of bag open. Sprinkle with additional French Fried Onions, if desired. *Makes 4 to 6 servings*

Mushrooms with Paprika and Sour Cream

2 tablespoons butter
1 bunch scallions, including green top (about 1 cup), sliced
1 pound white mushrooms, quartered
1/2 teaspoon salt
1/4 teaspoon ground black pepper
1 teaspoon flour
1 tablespoon sweet paprika
1/2 cup vegetable broth
1/2 cup sour cream

Heat butter in large skillet over high heat. Add scallions and mushrooms. Sauté 10 minutes, or until the mushrooms begin to color. Stir in salt and pepper. Sprinkle paprika and flour over mushrooms. Add broth and bring to a boil; reduce heat to low. Cover and simmer covered 4 minutes. Stir in sour cream just until heated. *Makes 2 or 3 servings*

Favorite recipe from **Mushroom Council**

Moist & Savory Stuffing

1-3/4 cups Swanson® Chicken Broth (Regular, Natural Goodness™ or Certified Organic)
Generous dash ground black pepper
1 stalk celery, coarsely chopped (about 1/2 cup)
1 small onion, coarsely chopped (about 1/4 cup)
4 cups Pepperidge Farm® Herb Seasoned Stuffing

1. Heat the broth, black pepper, celery and onion in a 2-quart saucepan over high heat to a boil. Reduce the heat to low. Cover and cook for 5 minutes or until the vegetables are tender.

2. Add the stuffing and stir lightly to coat.
Makes 4 cups

Scalloped Potatoes with Gorgonzola

New York Deli-Style Tuna

New York Deli-Style Tuna

(pictured above)

1 (3-ounce) STARKIST Flavor Fresh Pouch® Tuna
   (Albacore)
1 hard-cooked egg, minced
3 tablespoons minced celery
1 tablespoon chopped ripe olives
3 to 4 tablespoons mayonnaise
2 teaspoons mustard (optional)
1 tablespoon drained capers (optional)
3 New York style bagels, split
3 ounces cream cheese, softened
   Baby kosher dill pickles, thinly sliced
      lengthwise
   Thinly sliced red onion rings

In medium bowl, combine tuna, egg, celery, olives
and mayonnaise. Stir in mustard and capers, if
desired; blend well. Chill.

To serve, toast bagels; spread each half with
1/2 ounce cream cheese. Top each with 3 pickle
slices, about 3 tablespoons tuna mixture and red
onion rings; serve open face.   *Makes 6 servings*

Thai Portabella Wraps

4 medium (about 4 ounces each) portabella
   mushrooms, stems and gills removed
1 large sweet onion
2 tablespoons sesame oil
1/4 cup Thai peanut stir-fry and dipping sauce
2 cups coleslaw mix (from a 6-ounce bag)
1/2 cup chopped sweet red bell pepper
1/3 cup chopped fresh cilantro
4 large (10-inch) tomato or spinach flour tortilla
   wraps, warmed

Cut portabella mushrooms into 1/2-inch-thick slices.
Cut onion in half crosswise and then slice. In a
12-inch skillet (preferably nonstick), over medium-
high heat, heat oil. Add mushrooms and onion; cook
and stir until tender, about 8 minutes. Stir in Thai
peanut sauce; cook and stir until hot and flavors are
blended, about 2 minutes. Meanwhile, in a bowl,
combine coleslaw, bell pepper and cilantro. Spoon
an equal amount of the mushroom mixture down
the center of each wrap. Spoon coleslaw mixture on
one side of the mushroom mixture. Fold in sides of
each tortilla and roll up. To serve, cut each wrap in
half crosswise on the diagonal. Serve with
additional Thai peanut sauce, if desired.

Makes 4 servings

Favorite recipe from **Mushroom Council**

Warm Bacon and Chicken Salad Sandwiches

1 (10-ounce) can HORMEL® chunk breast of
   chicken, drained and flaked
1/2 cup mayonnaise or salad dressing
1/3 cup diced celery
1/4 cup minced onion
1/2 teaspoon lemon juice
1/2 teaspoon Worcestershire sauce
1/8 teaspoon ground black pepper
   Leaf lettuce
4 slices whole wheat bread, toasted
1/4 cup shredded carrot
1/4 cup HORMEL® real bacon bits

In small saucepan, combine chicken, mayonnaise,
celery, onion, lemon juice, Worcestershire sauce,
and pepper. Heat until warm. Place lettuce on toast.
Spread chicken mixture over lettuce. Top with
shredded carrot and bacon.   *Makes 4 servings*

Philly Cheesesteak Sandwiches

(pictured below)

> 1 box (1 pound 5 ounces) frozen thin beef
>   sandwich steaks
> 1 tablespoon olive oil
> 2 large sweet onions, halved and thinly sliced
> 1 large red bell pepper, cut into 1/4-inch strips
> 1/4 teaspoon salt
> 1/8 teaspoon ground black pepper
> 1 jar (1 pound) RAGÚ® Cheesy! Double Cheddar
>   Sauce
> 4 hoagie rolls, split

In 12-inch nonstick skillet, cook steaks, 2 at a time, over medium-high heat, stirring occasionally and breaking into pieces, 2 minutes or until done. Remove from skillet; set aside and keep warm. Repeat with remaining steaks. Clean skillet.

In same skillet, heat olive oil over medium heat and cook onions and red pepper, stirring occasionally, 15 minutes or until onions are caramelized. Season with salt and pepper.

Return steaks to skillet with 1/2 of the Double Cheddar Sauce. Cook, stirring occasionally, 2 minutes or until heated through.

To serve, evenly divide steak mixture on rolls, then drizzle with remaining Double Cheddar Sauce, heated.   *Makes 4 servings*

Chicken Pizzawiches

> 1 package (12 ounces) frozen breaded chicken
>   breast patties
> 1 cup shredded mozzarella cheese
> 1 jar (14 ounces) spaghetti sauce
> 1/2 cup HOLLAND HOUSE® Red Cooking Wine
> 4 sandwich buns

MICROWAVE DIRECTIONS

Microwave chicken patties as directed on package. Top each piece of chicken with 1/4 cup mozzarella. Microwave at HIGH an additional 30 to 60 seconds. Place spaghetti sauce and cooking wine in microwavable bowl covered with waxed paper and microwave at HIGH 4 to 5 minutes, stirring once. Place chicken patties on buns; spoon sauce over patties.   *Makes 4 servings*

Philly Cheesesteak Sandwich

Roasted Ratatouille Wraps

(pictured at right)

6 cups assorted fresh vegetables,* cut into 1-inch
    chunks
3 tablespoons olive oil
1 small onion, chopped
1 jar (1 pound 10 ounces) RAGÚ® Chunky Pasta
    Sauce
6 flour tortillas
1-1/2 cups shredded mozzarella cheese (about
    6 ounces)

*Assorted fresh vegetables: use eggplant, bell pepper, yellow squash
and/or zucchini*

Preheat oven to 400°F. Line jelly roll pan with
nonstick foil and toss vegetables with 2 tablespoons
olive oil. Roast, stirring once, 35 minutes or until
vegetables are tender.

In 12-inch nonstick skillet, heat remaining
1 tablespoon olive oil over medium heat and cook
onion, stirring occasionally, 4 minutes or until
tender. Add roasted vegetables and Pasta Sauce and
simmer, stirring occasionally, 5 minutes or until
heated through and slightly thickened.

Evenly spoon onto tortillas, then sprinkle with
cheese. Roll. *Makes 6 servings*

Smoked Chicken Salad with Dried Cherries and Onions

(pictured on page 80)

4-1/2 cups diced smoked chicken
2-1/4 cups diced sweet onions
2-1/4 cups diced dried tart cherries
    2 cups mayonnaise
1-1/2 cups diced celery
1-1/2 cups pecan pieces, lightly toasted
    1/2 cup fresh minced basil
    3 tablespoons fresh orange juice
    1 teaspoon orange zest
    3/4 teaspoon salt
    3/4 teaspoon black pepper

Place all ingredients in mixing bowl; stir gently until
well combined. Refrigerate until ready to prepare
sandwiches.
    Makes 12 sandwiches (9 cups chicken salad)

Favorite recipe from **National Onion Association**

Focaccia Sandwich

1 loaf Focaccia
2 tablespoons Italian dressing
6 slices provolone cheese
8 ounces deli honey ham
1 green pepper, sliced
1 (6-ounce) jar marinated artichoke hearts,
    drained and sliced
1/3 cup marinated sun-dried tomatoes, drained
1 teaspoon dried basil
6 slices Muenster cheese

Preheat oven to 375°F.

Cut Focaccia into 6 serving pieces. Slice each piece
lengthwise; spread Italian dressing on cut surfaces.

Place bottom layer of each serving piece, cut side
up, on large sheet of aluminum foil. Layer with
provolone cheese, ham, pepper strips, artichoke
hearts and sun-dried tomatoes. Sprinkle with basil.
Top with Muenster cheese and remaining half of
Focaccia; wrap with foil. Bake about 20 minutes or
until sandwich is hot and cheese is melted.
    Makes 6 servings

Favorite recipe from **Wheat Foods Council**

Garlic Roast Beef Subs

2 cups thinly sliced onions
3 tablespoons *French's®* Worcestershire Sauce
1 container (4 ounces) garlic-flavored cheese
    spread
4 sandwich rolls, split in half and toasted
12 ounces sliced deli roast beef

1. Melt *1 tablespoon butter* in medium skillet over
medium-high heat. Add onions; cook and stir
5 minutes or until tender. Add Worcestershire;
cook 2 minutes.

2. Spread about *1 tablespoon* cheese on each half of
rolls. Broil 30 seconds or until cheese begins to
brown. Layer roast beef and onions on bottoms of
rolls. Cover with top halves. *Makes 4 servings*

Roasted Ratatouille Wraps

Honey Muffins

(pictured at right)

1 can (8 ounces) DOLE® Crushed Pineapple
1-1/2 cups wheat bran cereal (not flakes)
2/3 cup buttermilk
1 egg, lightly beaten
1/3 cup chopped pecans or walnuts
3 tablespoons vegetable oil
1/2 cup honey, divided
2/3 cup whole wheat flour
1/2 teaspoon baking soda
1/8 teaspoon salt

Combine undrained crushed pineapple, cereal and buttermilk in large bowl. Let stand 10 minutes until cereal has absorbed liquid. Stir in egg, pecans, oil and 1/4 cup honey. Combine flour, baking soda and salt in small bowl. Stir into bran mixture until just moistened. Spoon one-half batter into 6 prepared cups,* filling to the top.

Microwave at HIGH (100%) for 3-1/2 to 4 minutes, rotating pan 1/2 turn after 1-1/2 minutes. Muffins are done when they look dry and set on top. Remove from oven; immediately spoon 1 teaspoon of remaining honey over each muffin. Remove to cooling rack after honey has been absorbed. Repeat procedure with remaining batter and honey. Serve warm. *Makes 12 muffins*

*Line six microwavable muffin cups or six 6-ounce microwavable custard cups with double thickness paper baking cups. (Outer cup will absorb moisture so inner cup sticks to cooked muffin.)

Quick Cinnamon Sticky Buns

1 cup packed light brown sugar, divided
10 tablespoons butter, softened and divided
1 package (16 ounces) hot roll mix
2 tablespoons granulated sugar
1 cup hot water (120° to 130°F)
1 egg
1-2/3 cups (10-ounce package) HERSHEY'S Cinnamon Chips

1. Lightly grease two 9-inch round baking pans. Combine 1/2 cup brown sugar and 4 tablespoons butter in small bowl with pastry blender; sprinkle mixture evenly on bottom of prepared pans. Set aside.

2. Combine contents of hot roll mix package, including yeast packet, and granulated sugar in large bowl. Using spoon, stir in water, 2 tablespoons butter

and egg until dough pulls away from sides of bowl. Turn dough onto lightly floured surface. With lightly floured hands, shape into ball. Knead 5 minutes or until smooth, using additional flour if necessary.

3. To shape: Using lightly floured rolling pin, roll into 15×12-inch rectangle. Spread with remaining 4 tablespoons butter. Sprinkle with remaining 1/2 cup brown sugar and cinnamon chips, pressing lightly into dough. Starting with 12-inch side, roll tightly as for jelly roll; seal edges.

4. Cut into 1-inch-wide slices with floured knife. Arrange 6 slices, cut sides down, in each prepared pan. Cover with towel; let rise in warm place until doubled, about 30 minutes.

5. Heat oven to 350°F. Uncover rolls. Bake 25 to 30 minutes or until golden brown. Cool 2 minutes in pan; with knife, loosen around edges of pan. Invert onto serving plates. Serve warm or at room temperature. *Makes 12 cinnamon buns*

Cheese Scones

1-1/2 cups all-purpose flour
1-1/2 cups uncooked quick-cooking oats
1/4 cup packed brown sugar
1 tablespoon baking powder
1 teaspoon cream of tartar
1/2 teaspoon salt
1/2 cup (2 ounces) finely shredded Wisconsin Cheddar cheese
2/3 cup butter, melted
1/3 cup milk
1 egg

Preheat oven to 425°F. Stir together flour, oats, brown sugar, baking powder, cream of tartar and salt in large bowl. Stir in cheese. Beat together butter, milk and egg in small bowl. Add to dry ingredients, stirring just until mixed. Shape dough into ball; pat onto lightly floured surface to form 8-inch circle. Cut into 8 to 12 wedges. Bake on buttered baking sheet 12 to 15 minutes until light golden brown. *Makes 8 to 12 scones*

Favorite recipe from **Wisconsin Milk Marketing Board**

Honey Muffins

Main Dishes

Louisiana Seafood Bake

(pictured at left)

1 can (14-1/2 ounces) whole tomatoes, undrained and
   cut up
1 can (8 ounces) tomato sauce
1 cup water
1 cup sliced celery
2/3 cup uncooked regular rice
1-1/3 cups *French's®* French Fried Onions, divided
1 teaspoon *Frank's® RedHot®* Original Cayenne Pepper
   Sauce
1/2 teaspoon garlic powder
1/4 teaspoon dried oregano, crumbled
1/4 teaspoon dried thyme, crumbled
1/2 pound white fish, thawed if frozen and cut into 1-inch
   chunks
1 can (4 ounces) shrimp, drained
1/3 cup sliced pitted ripe olives
1/4 cup (1 ounce) grated Parmesan cheese

Preheat oven to 375°F. In 1-1/2-quart casserole, combine
tomatoes, tomato sauce, water, celery, uncooked rice, *2/3 cup*
French Fried Onions and seasonings. Bake, covered, at 375°F
for 20 minutes. Stir in fish, shrimp and olives. Bake, covered,
20 minutes or until heated through. Top with cheese and
remaining *2/3 cup* onions; bake, uncovered, 3 minutes or until
onions are golden brown.   *Makes 4 servings*

Microwave Directions: In 2-quart microwave-safe casserole,
prepare rice mixture as above. Cook, covered, on HIGH
15 minutes, stirring rice halfway through cooking time. Add
fish, shrimp and olives. Cook, covered, 12 to 14 minutes or
until rice is cooked. Stir casserole halfway through cooking
time. Top with cheese and remaining *2/3 cup* onions; cook,
uncovered, 1 minute. Let stand 5 minutes.

Clockwise from top left: *Pesto-Crumbed
Australian Lamb Loin Chops with Tomato-Mint
Salad (p. 148), Louisiana Seafood Bake, Texas
Barbecued Ribs (p. 174) and Easy Cheese &
Tomato Macaroni (p. 142)*

Savory Dill Chicken

(pictured at right)

2 tablespoons I CAN'T BELIEVE IT'S NOT
BUTTER!® Spread
1-1/2 pounds boneless, skinless chicken breast halves
1 cup water
1 package KNORR® Recipe Classics™ Vegetable
or Spring Vegetable recipe mix
1/4 teaspoon dried dill weed
1/2 cup sour cream

• In large skillet, melt I Can't Believe It's Not Butter!®
Spread over medium-high heat and brown chicken,
turning occasionally, 5 minutes.

• Stir in water, recipe mix and dill weed. Bring to a
boil over high heat. Reduce heat to low and simmer
covered, stirring occasionally, 10 minutes or until
chicken is thoroughly cooked. Remove chicken to
serving platter and keep warm.

• Remove skillet from heat; stir in sour cream.
Spoon sauce over chicken and serve, if desired, with
noodles. *Makes 4 to 6 servings*

Southwest Skillet

3/4 pound ground beef
1 tablespoon chili powder
1 can Campbell's® Beefy Mushroom Soup
1/4 cup water
1 can (about 14-1/2 ounces) whole peeled
tomatoes, cut up
1 can (about 15 ounces) kidney beans, rinsed
and drained
3/4 cup uncooked instant white rice
1/2 cup shredded Cheddar cheese
Tortilla chips

1. Cook the beef with chili powder in a 10-inch
skillet over medium-high heat until it's well
browned, stirring frequently to break up meat. Pour
off any fat.

2. Stir the soup, water, tomatoes and beans into the
skillet. Heat to a boil. Reduce the heat to low. Cover
and cook for 10 minutes.

3. Stir in the rice. Cover the skillet and remove from
the heat. Let stand for 5 minutes. Fluff the rice with
a fork. Top with the cheese. Serve with the chips.
Makes 4 servings

Creamy Cuban Mojo Pork Grill

1 cup HELLMANN'S® or BEST FOODS® Real
Mayonnaise
2 cloves garlic, finely chopped
1 small jalapeño pepper, seeds and ribs removed
then finely chopped
2 tablespoons orange juice
1 tablespoon lime juice
1/2 teaspoon ground cumin
8 pork chops

1. In medium bowl, combine all ingredients except
chops. Reserve 1/2 cup mayonnaise mixture.

2. Season chops, if desired, with salt and ground
black pepper. Grill or broil chops, turning once and
brushing frequently with remaining mayonnaise
mixture, until chops are done. Serve with reserved
mayonnaise mixture. *Makes 8 servings*

Cheddar and Mustard-Topped
Broiled Fish

1 large or 2 small halibut or cod steaks
Olive oil
1 large egg white
1/4 cup grated CABOT® 50% Light Cheddar
1 tablespoon spicy brown mustard
1 tablespoon chopped green onions

1. Preheat broiler.

2. Brush both sides of fish lightly with oil. Set wire
rack on baking sheet and place fish on top.

3. Broil about 2 to 3 inches from heat for 5 minutes.
Turn over and continue broiling until just opaque in
center, 6 to 8 minutes longer.

4. In medium bowl with electric mixer, beat egg
white until stiff. Fold in cheese, mustard and green
onions. Spread mixture over top of fish.

5. Return to broiler until topping is golden, about
1-1/2 minutes longer. *Makes 2 servings*

Savory Dill Chicken

Italian Chicken Sauté

(pictured at right)

2 tablespoons olive or vegetable oil
1 pound boneless, skinless chicken breast halves, cut into strips
1/2 cup chopped green bell pepper
1/2 cup chopped onion
1 large clove garlic, minced
1 cup sliced fresh mushrooms
2 medium zucchini, sliced (about 1 cup)
1 can (14.5 ounces) CONTADINA® Recipe Ready Diced Tomatoes, undrained
2 tablespoons capers
1 tablespoon chopped fresh basil *or* 1 teaspoon dried basil leaves, crushed
1/2 teaspoon Italian herb seasoning
1/4 teaspoon salt
1/8 teaspoon crushed red pepper flakes
1 tablespoon cornstarch

1. Heat oil in large skillet. Add chicken, bell pepper, onion and garlic; sauté for 3 to 4 minutes or until chicken is lightly browned.

2. Add mushrooms and zucchini; sauté for 2 to 3 minutes or until zucchini are crisp-tender.

3. Drain tomatoes, reserving juice in small bowl. Add tomatoes, capers, basil, Italian seasoning, salt and red pepper flakes to skillet.

4. Add cornstarch into reserved tomato juice; mix well. Stir into mixture in skillet. Cook, stirring constantly, until liquid is thickened. Serve over hot cooked rice, if desired.   *Makes 4 servings*

Zesty Onion Meatloaf

2 pounds ground beef
1-1/3 cups *French's®* French Fried Onions
1 cup spaghetti sauce, divided
1/2 cup bread crumbs
1/4 cup *French's®* Worcestershire Sauce
2 eggs

1. Preheat oven to 350°F. Thoroughly mix beef, *2/3 cup* French Fried Onions, *1/2 cup* sauce, bread crumbs, Worcestershire Sauce and eggs in large bowl.

2. Shape into loaf in baking dish. Bake 1 hour or until thoroughly cooked and internal temperature reaches 160°F; drain. Top with remaining *1/2 cup* sauce and *2/3 cup* onions. Bake 5 minutes or until onions are golden.   *Makes 6 to 8 servings*

Paradise Veg•All® Peppers

1 pound ground pork
1 can (20 ounces) pineapple tidbits, drained
1/2 cup slivered almonds
1 cup cooked rice
1 can (15 ounces) VEG•ALL® Original Mixed Vegetables, drained
1 jar (10 ounces) sweet and sour sauce
1 can (11 ounces) mandarin oranges, drained
1/2 teaspoon salt
1/4 teaspoon pepper
5 large green, red, or yellow peppers, cleaned and cut in half

Preheat oven to 350°F. In medium frying pan, cook ground pork until no longer pink, stirring to break into pieces. In medium mixing bowl, combine all ingredients except peppers. Divide mixture between the pepper halves and place in 9×13-inch pan. Bake for 35 to 45 minutes. Serve hot.

Makes 10 servings

Mandarin Orange Chicken

1/3 cup HOLLAND HOUSE® White Cooking Wine
3 ounces frozen orange juice concentrate, thawed
1/4 cup orange marmalade
1/2 teaspoon ground ginger
4 boneless chicken breast halves (about 1 pound)
1 can (11 ounces) mandarin orange segments, drained
1/2 cup green grapes, halved

Heat oven to 350°F. In 12×8-inch (2-quart) baking dish, combine cooking wine, concentrate, marmalade and ginger; mix well. Add chicken; turn to coat. Bake 45 to 60 minutes, or until chicken is tender and no longer pink in center, basting occasionally.* Add orange segments and grapes during last 5 minutes of cooking.

Makes 4 servings

Do not baste during last 5 minutes of cooking.

Italian Chicken Sauté

Italian Sausage and Peppers

(pictured at right)

3 cups (1-inch) bell pepper chunks, preferably a
    mix of red, yellow and green*
1 small onion, cut into thin wedges
3 garlic cloves, minced
4 links hot or mild Italian sausage (about
    1 pound)
1 cup pasta or marinara sauce
1/4 cup red wine or port
1 tablespoon cornstarch
1 tablespoon water
    Hot cooked spaghetti
1/4 cup grated Parmesan or Romano cheese

*Look for mixed bell pepper chunks at the supermarket salad bar.

SLOW COOKER DIRECTIONS
1. Coat 3-quart slow cooker with cooking spray.
Place bell peppers, onion and garlic in slow cooker.
Arrange sausage over vegetables. Combine pasta
sauce and wine; pour over sausage. Cover; cook on
LOW 8 to 9 hours or on HIGH 4 to 5 hours.

2. Transfer sausage to serving platter; cover with
foil to keep warm. Skim off and discard fat from
juices in slow cooker.

3. Turn heat to HIGH. Mix cornstarch with water
until smooth; add to slow cooker. Cook 15 minutes
or until sauce is thickened, stirring once. Serve
sauce over spaghetti and sausage; top with cheese.
Makes 4 servings

Chicken Pesto Pizza

2 teaspoons cornmeal
1 (12- to 14-inch) prepared pizza crust, uncooked
1/2 cup prepared pesto sauce
1/2 cup finely minced sun-dried tomatoes
1 (10-ounce) can HORMEL® chunk breast of
    chicken, drained and flaked
1 small bell pepper, thinly sliced into rings
1 cup shredded mozzarella cheese
1/4 cup grated Parmesan cheese
    Crushed red pepper flakes, if desired

Sprinkle cornmeal on bottom of pizza pan. Place
pizza crust over cornmeal. Spoon pesto sauce over
surface of crust. Top with remaining ingredients.
Bake at 400°F 12 to 15 minutes or until cheese is
melted and edges are lightly browned.
Makes 4 to 6 servings

Skillet Fiesta Chicken & Rice

1 tablespoon vegetable oil
4 skinless, boneless chicken breast halves
1 can (10-3/4 ounces) Campbell's® Condensed
    Tomato Soup (Regular or Healthy Request®)
1-1/3 cups water
1 teaspoon chili powder
1-1/2 cups uncooked instant white rice
1/4 cup shredded Cheddar cheese

1. Heat the oil in a 10-inch skillet over medium-high
heat. Add the chicken and cook for 10 minutes or
until it's well browned on both sides. Remove the
chicken and set aside. Pour off any fat.

2. Stir the soup, water and chili powder into the
skillet. Heat to a boil.

3. Stir in the rice. Place the chicken on the rice
mixture. Sprinkle chicken with additional chili
powder and the cheese. Reduce the heat to low.
Cover and cook for 5 minutes or until the chicken is
cooked through and the rice is tender. Stir the rice
mixture before serving.   *Makes 4 servings*

Swiss Chicken Gratin

1 (10-3/4-ounce) can condensed cream of
    mushroom, chicken or celery soup,
    undiluted
1/4 cup white wine, dry Vermouth or milk
1 (9- to 10-ounce) package fresh or frozen
    cooked chicken, thawed, cut into strips or
    chunks *or* 2 cups leftover rotisserie chicken,
    cut into chunks
1/4 cup sliced green onions
2 BAYS® English Muffins, cut into 1-inch chunks
1 cup shredded Swiss cheese
1/8 teaspoon ground nutmeg
    Paprika (optional)

Preheat oven to 375°F. Combine soup and wine in
large bowl; mix well. Add chicken and green onions;
mix well. Spread mixture into 1-1/2-quart (11×7-
inch) baking dish. Top with muffins and cheese.
Sprinkle nutmeg and paprika, if desired, over top of
casserole. Bake for 20 to 25 minutes or until golden
brown and bubbly.   *Makes 4 servings*

Italian Sausage and Peppers

Seafood Newburg Casserole

Texas Barbecued Ribs

(pictured on page 126)

1 cup GRANDMA'S® Molasses
1/2 cup coarse-grained mustard
2 tablespoons cider vinegar
2 teaspoons dry mustard
3-1/2 pounds pork loin baby back ribs or spareribs, cut into 6 sections

Prepare grill for direct cooking. In medium bowl, combine molasses, coarse-grained mustard, cider vinegar and dry mustard. When ready to cook, place ribs on grill, meaty side up, over medium-hot coals. Grill 1 to 1-1/4 hours or until meat is tender and starts to pull away from bone, basting frequently with sauce* during last 15 minutes of grilling. To serve, cut ribs apart carefully with knife and arrange on platter. *Makes 4 servings*

Do not baste during last 5 minutes of cooking.

Chicken Florentine

4 (6-ounce) skinless, boneless chicken breast halves
1/4 teaspoon salt
1/4 teaspoon freshly ground black pepper
1/2 cup Italian seasoned dry bread crumbs
1 egg, separated
1 (10-ounce) package frozen chopped spinach, thawed, well drained
1/8 teaspoon nutmeg
2 tablespoons olive oil
4 slices SARGENTO® Deli Style Sliced Mozzarella Cheese
1 cup prepared tomato basil or marinara spaghetti sauce, heated

1. Sprinkle chicken with salt and pepper. Place bread crumbs in a shallow plate. Beat egg white in a shallow bowl. Dip each chicken breast in egg white, letting excess drip off, roll lightly in crumbs, patting to coat well. (At this point, chicken may be covered and refrigerated up to 4 hours before cooking.)

2. Combine spinach, egg yolk and nutmeg; mix well. Heat oil in a large skillet (with cover) over medium-high heat until hot. Add chicken breasts; cook 3 minutes per side or until golden brown. Reduce heat to low. Top each chicken breast with 1/4 of spinach mixture and 1 slice of cheese. Cover skillet and continue cooking 6 minutes or until chicken is no longer pink in center. Spoon spaghetti sauce over chicken. *Makes 4 servings*

Seafood Newburg Casserole

(pictured above)

1 can (10-3/4 ounces) condensed cream of shrimp soup, undiluted
1/2 cup half-and-half cream
1 tablespoon dry sherry
1/4 teaspoon cayenne pepper
3 cups cooked rice
2 cans (6 ounces each) lump crabmeat, drained
1/4 pound medium raw shrimp, peeled and deveined
1/4 pound raw bay scallops
1 jar (4 ounces) pimientos, drained and chopped
1/4 cup finely chopped fresh parsley

1. Preheat oven to 350°F. Spray 2-1/2-quart casserole with nonstick cooking spray.

2. Whisk together soup, half-and-half cream, sherry and cayenne pepper in large bowl until blended. Add rice, crabmeat, shrimp, scallops and pimientos; toss well.

3. Transfer mixture to prepared casserole; sprinkle with parsley. Cover; bake about 25 minutes or until shrimp are pink and scallops are opaque. *Makes 6 servings*

Peachy Smothered Pork Chops

(pictured below)

      1 tablespoon vegetable oil
      1 small onion, finely minced
      1 (12-ounce) jar peach preserves
  2/3 cup *French's* Honey Mustard
      2 teaspoons grated peeled ginger root
  1/4 teaspoon ground nutmeg
      6 boneless pork chops, cut 1-inch thick

1. Heat oil in small saucepan; sauté onion until tender. Stir in peach preserves, mustard, ginger and nutmeg. Heat to boiling; simmer 5 minutes until flavors are blended. Transfer 3/4 cup sauce to bowl for basting. Reserve remaining sauce; keep warm.

2. Grill or broil chops over medium direct heat 20 minutes until barely pink in center, turning and basting often with sauce.

3. Serve chops with reserved sauce mixture.

Makes 6 servings

Alternate Method: For alternate skillet method, brown chops in skillet. Pour peach mixture over chops and simmer until no longer pink in center.

Citrus Spiced Pork Lo Mein

      6 ounces linguine
      4 teaspoons HERB-OX® chicken flavored
          bouillon, divided
      8 ounces pork tenderloin, halved lengthwise and
          cut into 1/4-inch strips
      2 teaspoons vegetable oil
      2 cups sliced bok choy
  3/4 cup water
  1/4 cup orange juice
      2 tablespoons soy sauce
      2 teaspoons sesame oil
  1/2 teaspoon red pepper flakes
      1 (11-ounce) can mandarin oranges, drained

Cook noodles according to package directions, adding 2 teaspoons of the bouillon to the cooking liquid. Meanwhile in wok or large skillet, stir-fry pork in hot vegetable oil for 3 minutes. Add bok choy and cook for an additional 3 to 4 minutes or until pork is cooked through and bok choy is crisp-tender. Add the water, orange juice, remaining bouillon, soy sauce, sesame oil and red pepper flakes to the pork mixture. Bring mixture to a boil. Stir in prepared noodles and stir for 1 minute. Remove mixture from heat and gently stir in oranges. *Makes 4 servings*

Peachy Smothered Pork Chop

Desserts

Fudgy Ripple Cake

(pictured at left)

1 package (18.25 ounces) yellow cake mix, plus ingredients
   to prepare mix
1 package (3 ounces) cream cheese, softened
2 tablespoons unsweetened cocoa powder
   Fudgy Glaze (recipe follows)
1/2 cup "M&M's"® Chocolate Mini Baking Bits

Preheat oven to 350°F. Lightly grease and flour 10-inch Bundt
or ring pan; set aside. Prepare cake mix as package directs. In
medium bowl combine 1-1/2 cups prepared batter, cream
cheese and cocoa powder until smooth. Pour half of yellow
batter into prepared pan. Drop spoonfuls of chocolate batter
over yellow batter in pan. Top with remaining yellow batter.
Bake about 45 minutes or until toothpick inserted near center
comes out clean. Cool completely on wire rack. Unmold cake
onto serving plate. Prepare Fudgy Glaze; spread over top of
cake, allowing some glaze to run over side. Sprinkle with
"M&M's"® Chocolate Mini Baking Bits. Store in tightly covered
container.   *Makes 10 servings*

Fudgy Glaze

1 square (1 ounce) semi-sweet chocolate
1 cup powdered sugar
1/3 cup unsweetened cocoa powder
3 tablespoons milk
1/2 teaspoon vanilla extract

Place chocolate in small microwave-safe bowl. Microwave at
HIGH 30 seconds; stir. Repeat as necessary until chocolate is
completely melted, stirring at 10-second intervals; set aside. In
medium bowl combine powdered sugar and cocoa powder.
Stir in milk, vanilla and melted chocolate until smooth.

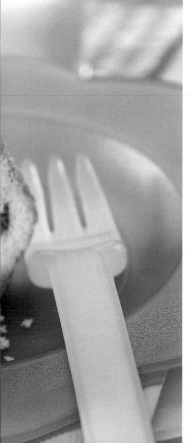

Clockwise from top left: *Strawberry Cheesecake
Pie (p. 204), Chocolate Pistachio Cookies (p.186),
Fudgy Ripple Cake and Chocolate-Topped Peanut
Bars (p.196)*

Scrumptious Apple Cake

(pictured at right)

        3 egg whites
  1-1/2 cups sugar
        1 cup unsweetened applesauce
        1 teaspoon vanilla
        2 cups all-purpose flour
        2 teaspoons ground cinnamon
        1 teaspoon baking soda
    1/4 teaspoon salt
        4 cups sliced cored peeled tart apples (McIntosh
            or Crispin)
          Yogurt Glaze (recipe follows)

Preheat oven to 350°F. Beat egg whites until slightly foamy; add sugar, applesauce and vanilla. Combine flour, cinnamon, baking soda and salt in separate bowl; add to applesauce mixture. Spread apples in 13×9-inch pan or 9-inch round springform pan sprayed with nonstick cooking spray. Spread batter over apples. Bake 35 to 40 minutes or until wooden toothpick inserted into center comes out clean; cool on wire rack. Prepare Yogurt Glaze; spread over cooled cake.   *Makes 15 to 20 servings*

Yogurt Glaze: Combine 1-1/2 cups plain or vanilla nonfat yogurt, 3 tablespoons brown sugar (or to taste) and 1 teaspoon vanilla or 1 teaspoon lemon juice. Stir together until smooth.

Favorite recipe from **New York Apple Association, Inc.**

Chocolate Glazed Citrus Poppy Seed Cake

        1 package (about 18 ounces) lemon cake mix
    1/3 cup poppy seed
    1/3 cup milk
        3 eggs
        1 container (8 ounces) plain lowfat yogurt
        1 teaspoon freshly grated lemon peel
          Chocolate Citrus Glaze (recipe follows)

1. Heat oven to 350°F. Grease and flour 12-cup fluted tube pan or 10-inch tube pan.

2. Combine cake mix, poppy seed, milk, eggs, yogurt and lemon peel in large bowl; beat until well blended. Pour batter into prepared pan.

3. Bake 40 to 45 minutes or until wooden pick inserted in center comes out clean. Cool 20 minutes; remove from pan to wire rack. Cool completely.

4. Prepare Chocolate Citrus Glaze; spoon over cake, allowing glaze to run down sides.
Makes 12 servings

Chocolate Citrus Glaze

        2 tablespoons butter or margarine
        2 tablespoons HERSHEY'S Cocoa or HERSHEY'S
            SPECIAL DARK™ Cocoa
        2 tablespoons water
        1 tablespoon orange-flavored liqueur (optional)
    1/2 teaspoon orange extract
  1-1/4 to 1-1/2 cups powdered sugar

Melt butter in small saucepan over medium heat; remove from heat. Stir in cocoa, water, liqueur, if desired, and orange extract. Whisk in 1-1/4 cups powdered sugar until smooth. If glaze is too thin, whisk in remaining 1/4 cup powdered sugar. Use immediately.

Tomato Soup Spice Cake

        1 box (about 18 ounces) spice cake mix
        1 can (10-3/4 ounces) Campbell's® Condensed
            Tomato Soup (Regular or Healthy Request®)
    1/2 cup water
        2 eggs
          Cream cheese frosting

1. Heat the oven to 350°F. Grease and lightly flour two 8- or 9-inch round cake pans

2. Beat the cake mix, soup, water and eggs following the package directions. Spoon the batter evenly between the prepared pans.

3. Bake for 25 minutes or until a toothpick inserted in the center comes out clean.

4. Cool in pans on wire racks for 10 minutes. Remove the cakes from the pans and cool them completely on the wire racks.

5. Fill and frost the cake with your favorite cream cheese frosting.   *Makes 12 servings*

Scrumptious Apple Cake

Mini Lemon Sandwich Cookies

Mini Lemon Sandwich Cookies

(pictured above)

2 cups all-purpose flour
1-1/4 cups (2-1/2 sticks) butter, softened, divided
1/3 cup whipping cream
1/2 cup granulated sugar, divided
1 teaspoon lemon peel
1/8 teaspoon lemon extract
3/4 cup confectioners' sugar
1 to 3 teaspoons lemon juice
1 teaspoon vanilla extract
Food coloring (optional)

1. For cookies, combine flour, 1 cup butter, cream, 1/4 cup granulated sugar, lemon peel and lemon extract in large bowl. Beat with electric mixer at medium speed 2 to 3 minutes or until well blended. Divide dough into thirds. Wrap each portion in waxed paper; refrigerate until firm.

2. Preheat oven to 375°F. Place remaining 1/4 cup granulated sugar in shallow bowl. Roll each portion of dough to 1/8-inch thickness on well-floured surface. Cut out dough with 1-1/2-inch round cookie cutter. Dip both sides of each cookie in sugar. Place

1 inch apart on ungreased cookie sheets; pierce several times with fork.

3. Bake 6 to 9 minutes or until cookies are slightly puffed but not brown. Cool 1 minute on cookie sheets; remove to wire racks to cool completely.

4. For filling, combine confectioners' sugar, remaining 1/4 cup butter, lemon juice and vanilla extract in medium bowl. Beat 1 to 2 minutes or until smooth. Tint with food coloring, if desired. Spread 1/2 teaspoon filling each on bottoms of half of cookies; top with remaining cookies.

Makes 4-1/2 dozen sandwich cookies

Cappuccino Caramels Royale

1 cup (2 sticks) butter
2 (1-ounce) squares unsweetened chocolate, chopped
2-1/4 cups firmly packed brown sugar
1 (14-ounce) can EAGLE BRAND® Sweetened Condensed Milk (NOT evaporated milk)
1 cup light corn syrup
1 tablespoon instant coffee crystals
1 cup chopped pecans or walnuts (optional)

1. Line 8-inch pan with foil, extending foil over edges of pan. Butter foil; set aside.

2. In heavy 3-quart saucepan, melt 1 cup butter and chocolate. Stir in brown sugar, EAGLE BRAND®, corn syrup and coffee crystals. Clip candy thermometer to side of pan. Cook over medium heat, stirring constantly, until thermometer reads 248°F (firm-ball stage*). Mixture should boil at moderate, steady rate, bubbling evenly over entire surface, to reach firm-ball stage, about 15 to 20 minutes.

3. Remove from heat. Remove thermometer. Immediately stir in nuts (optional). Quickly pour into prepared pan, spreading evenly with spoon. Cool.

4. When candy is firm, use foil to lift candy out of pan. Use buttered knife to cut into squares. Wrap each square in plastic wrap or place in candy cups if desired.

Makes about 3 pounds or 5 dozen caramels

*To test candy, spoon a few drops of the hot caramel into a cup of cold (but not icy) water. Use your fingers to form the drops into a ball. Remove the ball from the water. If it holds its shape but quickly flattens at room temperature, it has reached firm-ball stage. If the mixture hasn't reached the correct stage, continue cooking and re-test again with fresh cold water and a clean spoon.

Individual Chocolate Soufflés

(pictured below)

Unsalted butter
5 tablespoons granulated sugar, divided
4 ounces semisweet chocolate, chopped
2 ounces cream cheese, softened
2 tablespoons milk
2 eggs, separated, at room temperature
Pinch salt
Confectioners' sugar

1. Grease 2 (10-ounce) custard cups with butter; coat with 1 tablespoon granulated sugar.

2. Make collars for custard cups: fold 16-inch-long piece of foil in half lengthwise, and fold in half again. Use butter to grease half of it lengthwise. Sprinkle buttered part with 1-1/2 teaspoons sugar. Wrap foil around custard cup, buttered side in; allow buttered half to extend above the rim 1 inch. If necessary, secure with masking tape. Repeat for second collar.

3. Preheat oven to 350°F. Place baking pan in oven. Microwave chocolate, cream cheese and milk in microwavable bowl on HIGH 1 minute. Stir until smooth. If mixture is not completely melted, return to microwave and heat in 30-second intervals, stirring after each interval. Allow mixture to cool,; stir in egg yolks and blend well.

4. Beat egg whites in medium bowl with electric mixer at high speed until frothy. Add salt. Gradually add remaining 3 tablespoons sugar, beating constantly, until stiff peaks form.

5. Gently fold whites into chocolate mixture in 3 additions. Divide between custard cups.

6. Place custard cups on preheated baking pan. Bake 35 to 40 minutes or until puffed and toothpick inserted into centers comes out clean. Sprinkle with confectioners' sugar. Remove collars and serve immediately (soufflés deflate as they cool).

Makes 2 servings

Tip: Place soufflés in the oven just before serving your meal; they will be ready when it's time for dessert and coffee.

Individual Chocolate Soufflé

Mixed Berry Crisp

Mixed Berry Crisp

(pictured above)

    2 teaspoons plus 1 tablespoon granulated sugar,
      divided
    1 tablespoon cornstarch*
    2 cups mixed berries, thawed if frozen
  1/2 cup old-fashioned oats
  1/4 cup packed brown sugar
    2 tablespoons all-purpose flour
  1/2 teaspoon cinnamon
  1/8 teaspoon ground ginger
  1/8 teaspoon salt
    3 tablespoons cold butter

Increase to 2 tablespoons if using frozen berries.

1. Preheat oven to 375°F.

2. Combine 2 teaspoons granulated sugar and cornstarch in medium bowl. Add berries; toss to coat evenly. Divide berry mixture between 2 (5-inch) heart-shaped pie plates or 5-inch baking dishes.

3. For topping, combine oats, brown sugar, flour, remaining 1 tablespoon granulated sugar, cinnamon, ginger and salt in small bowl. Cut in butter using

pastry blender or two knives, until mixture resembles coarse crumbs. Sprinkle topping evenly over berries. Bake 20 to 25 minutes or until topping is golden brown and berries are bubbling around edges. Serve warm. *Makes 2 servings*

Strawberry Cheesecake Pie

(pictured on page 184)

    1 *prepared* 9-inch (6 ounces) graham cracker
      crumb crust
  2/3 cup (5-fluid-ounce can) NESTLÉ®
      CARNATION® Evaporated Fat Free Milk
    1 package (8 ounces) fat-free cream cheese,
      softened
    1 large egg
  1/2 cup granulated sugar
    2 tablespoons all-purpose flour
    1 teaspoon grated lemon peel
1-1/2 to 2 cups halved fresh strawberries
    3 tablespoons strawberry jelly, warmed

PREHEAT oven to 325°F.

PLACE evaporated milk, cream cheese, egg, sugar, flour and lemon peel in blender; cover. Blend until smooth. Pour into crust.

BAKE for 35 to 40 minutes or until center is set. Cool completely in pan on wire rack. Arrange strawberries on top of pie; drizzle with jelly. Refrigerate before serving. *Makes 8 servings*

Helpful Hint

Most cobblers and crisps are best served warm or at room temperature the day they are made. Leftovers should be covered and stored in refrigerator for up to two days. Reheat them, covered, in a 350°F oven until warm.

Mini Chip Snowball Cookies

(pictured below)

1-1/2 cups (3 sticks) butter or margarine, softened
3/4 cup powdered sugar
1 tablespoon vanilla extract
1/2 teaspoon salt
3 cups all-purpose flour
2 cups (12-ounce package) NESTLÉ® TOLL
    HOUSE® Semi-Sweet Chocolate Mini Morsels
1/2 cup finely chopped nuts
    Powdered sugar

PREHEAT oven to 375°F.

BEAT butter, sugar, vanilla extract and salt in large mixer bowl until creamy. Gradually beat in flour; stir in morsels and nuts. Shape level tablespoons of dough into 1-1/4-inch balls. Place on ungreased baking sheets.

BAKE for 10 to 12 minutes or until cookies are set and lightly browned. Remove from oven. Sift powdered sugar over hot cookies on baking sheets. Cool on baking sheets for 10 minutes; remove to wire racks to cool completely. Sprinkle with additional powdered sugar, if desired. Store in airtight containers.   *Makes about 5 dozen cookies*

Chocolate and Coconut Cream Fondue

1 can (15 ounces) cream of coconut
1 fluid ounce (2 tablespoons) rum (optional) or
    1 teaspoon rum extract
1 package (12 ounces) semi-sweet chocolate
    pieces
    Suggested Dippers: Assorted Pepperidge Farm®
    Cookies, Pepperidge Farm® Graham Giant
    Goldfish® Baked Snack Crackers, whole
    strawberries, banana chunks, dried pineapple
    pieces and/or fresh pineapple chunks

1. Stir the cream of coconut, rum, if desired and chocolate in a 2-quart saucepan. Heat over medium heat until the chocolate melts, stirring occasionally.

2. Pour the chocolate mixture into a fondue pot or slow cooker.

3. Serve warm with the Suggested Dippers.

Makes 3 cups

Leftover Tip: Any remaining fondue can be used as an ice cream or dessert topping. Cover and refrigerate in an airtight container. Reheat in saucepot until warm.

Mini Chip Snowball Cookies

Pecan Pie Bars

(pictured at right)

2 cups all-purpose flour
1/4 cup firmly packed brown sugar
1/2 cup (1 stick) cold butter
1-1/2 cups chopped pecans
1 (14-ounce) can EAGLE BRAND® Sweetened
    Condensed Milk (NOT evaporated milk)
3 eggs, beaten
2 tablespoons lemon juice

1. Preheat oven to 350°F. In medium bowl, combine flour and brown sugar; cut in butter until crumbly.

2. Press mixture on bottom of 13×9-inch baking pan. Bake 10 to 15 minutes or until crust is light golden.

3. In large bowl, combine pecans, EAGLE BRAND®, eggs and lemon juice; pour over crust.

4. Bake 25 minutes or until filling is set. Cool. Cut into bars. Store covered at room temperature.

Makes about 3 dozen bars

Double Decadence Chocolate Chip Brownies

1 cup granulated sugar
1 stick plus 3 tablespoons margarine or butter,
    softened
2 eggs
1 teaspoon vanilla
2 cups (12 ounces) semisweet chocolate pieces,
    divided
1-1/4 cups all-purpose flour
1 cup QUAKER® Oats (quick or old fashioned,
    uncooked)
1 teaspoon baking powder
1/2 cup chopped nuts (optional)
    Powdered sugar

Heat oven to 350°F. Lightly grease 13×9-inch baking pan. Beat sugar, margarine, eggs and vanilla until smooth. Add 1 cup chocolate pieces, melted;* mix well. Add flour, oats, baking powder, remaining 1 cup chocolate pieces and nuts; mix well. Spread into prepared pan. Bake 25 to 30 minutes or until brownies just begin to pull away from sides of pan. Cool completely. Sprinkle with powdered sugar, if desired. Cut into bars.   *Makes 2 dozen brownies*

*To melt 1 cup chocolate pieces: Microwave at HIGH 1 to 2 minutes, stirring every 30 seconds until smooth. Or, heat in heavy saucepan over low heat, stirring until smooth.

Brownie Ice Cream Pie

1 (21-ounce) package DUNCAN HINES® Chewy
    Fudge Brownie Mix
2 eggs
1/2 cup vegetable oil
1/4 cup water
3/4 cup semisweet chocolate chips
1 (9-inch) unbaked pastry crust
1 (10-ounce) package frozen sweetened sliced
    strawberries
    Vanilla ice cream

1. Preheat oven to 350°F.

2. Combine brownie mix, eggs, oil and water in large bowl. Stir with spoon until well blended, about 50 strokes. Stir in chocolate chips. Spoon into crust. Bake at 350°F for 40 to 45 minutes or until set. Cool completely. Purée strawberries in food processor or blender. Cut pie into wedges. Serve with ice cream and puréed strawberries.   *Makes 8 servings*

Peach Cobbler

2 cans (21 ounces each) peach pie filling
1-1/2 cups all-purpose flour
1/3 cup sugar
2 teaspoons baking powder
1 teaspoon ground cinnamon
1/2 cup HELLMANN'S® or BEST FOODS® Real
    Mayonnaise
1/2 cup milk

1. Preheat oven to 375°F.

2. Evenly spread peach filling in 8×8-inch baking dish.

3. In medium bowl combine flour, sugar, baking powder and cinnamon. Stir in Hellmann's or Best Foods Real Mayonnaise and milk just until combined. Evenly spoon over filling.

4. Bake 40 minutes until golden and bubbly.

Makes 8 servings

Pecan Pie Bars

METRIC CONVERSION CHART

VOLUME MEASUREMENTS (dry)

$\frac{1}{8}$ teaspoon = 0.5 mL
$\frac{1}{4}$ teaspoon = 1 mL
$\frac{1}{2}$ teaspoon = 2 mL
$\frac{3}{4}$ teaspoon = 4 mL
1 teaspoon = 5 mL
1 tablespoon = 15 mL
2 tablespoons = 30 mL
$\frac{1}{4}$ cup = 60 mL
$\frac{1}{3}$ cup = 75 mL
$\frac{1}{2}$ cup = 125 mL
$\frac{2}{3}$ cup = 150 mL
$\frac{3}{4}$ cup = 175 mL
1 cup = 250 mL
2 cups = 1 pint = 500 mL
3 cups = 750 mL
4 cups = 1 quart = 1 L

VOLUME MEASUREMENTS (fluid)

1 fluid ounce (2 tablespoons) = 30 mL
4 fluid ounces ($\frac{1}{2}$ cup) = 125 mL
8 fluid ounces (1 cup) = 250 mL
12 fluid ounces ($1\frac{1}{2}$ cups) = 375 mL
16 fluid ounces (2 cups) = 500 mL

WEIGHTS (mass)

$\frac{1}{2}$ ounce = 15 g
1 ounce = 30 g
3 ounces = 90 g
4 ounces = 120 g
8 ounces = 225 g
10 ounces = 285 g
12 ounces = 360 g
16 ounces = 1 pound = 455 g

DIMENSIONS

$\frac{1}{16}$ inch = 2 mm
$\frac{1}{8}$ inch = 3 mm
$\frac{1}{4}$ inch = 6 mm
$\frac{1}{2}$ inch = 1.5 cm
$\frac{3}{4}$ inch = 2 cm
1 inch = 2.5 cm

OVEN TEMPERATURES

250°F = 120°C
275°F = 140°C
300°F = 150°C
325°F = 160°C
350°F = 180°C
375°F = 190°C
400°F = 200°C
425°F = 220°C
450°F = 230°C

BAKING PAN SIZES

Utensil	Size in Inches/Quarts	Metric Volume	Size in Centimeters
Baking or Cake Pan (square or rectangular)	$8 \times 8 \times 2$	2 L	$20 \times 20 \times 5$
	$9 \times 9 \times 2$	2.5 L	$23 \times 23 \times 5$
	$12 \times 8 \times 2$	3 L	$30 \times 20 \times 5$
	$13 \times 9 \times 2$	3.5 L	$33 \times 23 \times 5$
Loaf Pan	$8 \times 4 \times 3$	1.5 L	$20 \times 10 \times 7$
	$9 \times 5 \times 3$	2 L	$23 \times 13 \times 7$
Round Layer Cake Pan	$8 \times 1\frac{1}{2}$	1.2 L	20×4
	$9 \times 1\frac{1}{2}$	1.5 L	23×4
Pie Plate	$8 \times 1\frac{1}{4}$	750 mL	20×3
	$9 \times 1\frac{1}{4}$	1 L	23×3
Baking Dish or Casserole	1 quart	1 L	—
	$1\frac{1}{2}$ quart	1.5 L	—
	2 quart	2 L	—